P9-CQI-611

Tatsuki Fujimoto

I love chainsaws!

Tatsuki Fujimoto won Honorable Mention in the November 2013 Shueisha Crown Newcomers' Awards for his debut one-shot story *Love Is Blind*. His first series, *Fire Punch*, ran for eight volumes. *Chainsaw Man* began serialization in 2018 in *Weekly Shonen Jump*.

CHAINSAW MAN

1

SHONEN JUMP Manga Edition

Story & Art **TATSUKI FUJIMOTO**

Translation/AMANDA HALEY
Touch-Up Art & Lettering/SABRINA HEEP
Design/JULIAN [JR] ROBINSON
Editor/ALEXIS KIRSCH

CHAINSAW MAN © 2018 by Tatsuki Fujimoto
All rights reserved.
First published in Japan in 2018 by SHUEISHA Inc., Tokyo.
English translation rights arranged by SHUEISHA Inc.

The stories, characters and incidents mentioned in this publication are entirely fictional.

No portion of this book may be reproduced or transmitted in any form or by any means without written permission from the copyright holders.

Printed in the U.S.A.

Published by VIZ Media, LLC
P.O. Box 77010
San Francisco, CA 94107

10 9 8 7
First printing, October 2020
Seventh printing, October 2021

YOU'RE READING THE WRONG WAY!

CHAINSAW MAN

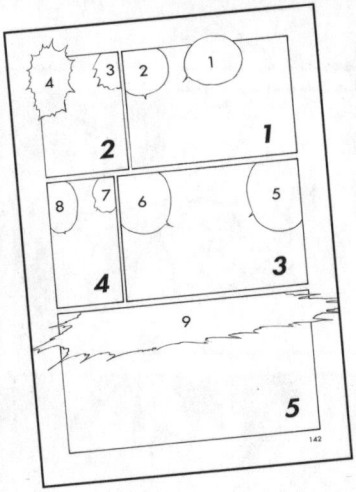

Chainsaw Man reads from right to left, starting in the upper-right corner. Japanese is read from right to left, meaning that action, sound effects and word-balloon order are completely reversed from English order.

HEY, DON'T THROW AWAY YOUR APPLE PEELS.
THESE ARE EDIBLE!
IF YOU DON'T WANT THE SKIN, GIVE IT TO ME.
I'LL EAT IT.
GIMME YOUR SCABS.
I CAN EAT THOSE.
WHY NOT?! THEY'RE NUTRI-TIOUS!
WHAT KIND OF LIFE HAVE YOU LIVED?
NO WAY.

Chain
saw
man

TO BE CONTINUED...

BL
VRE
EEE

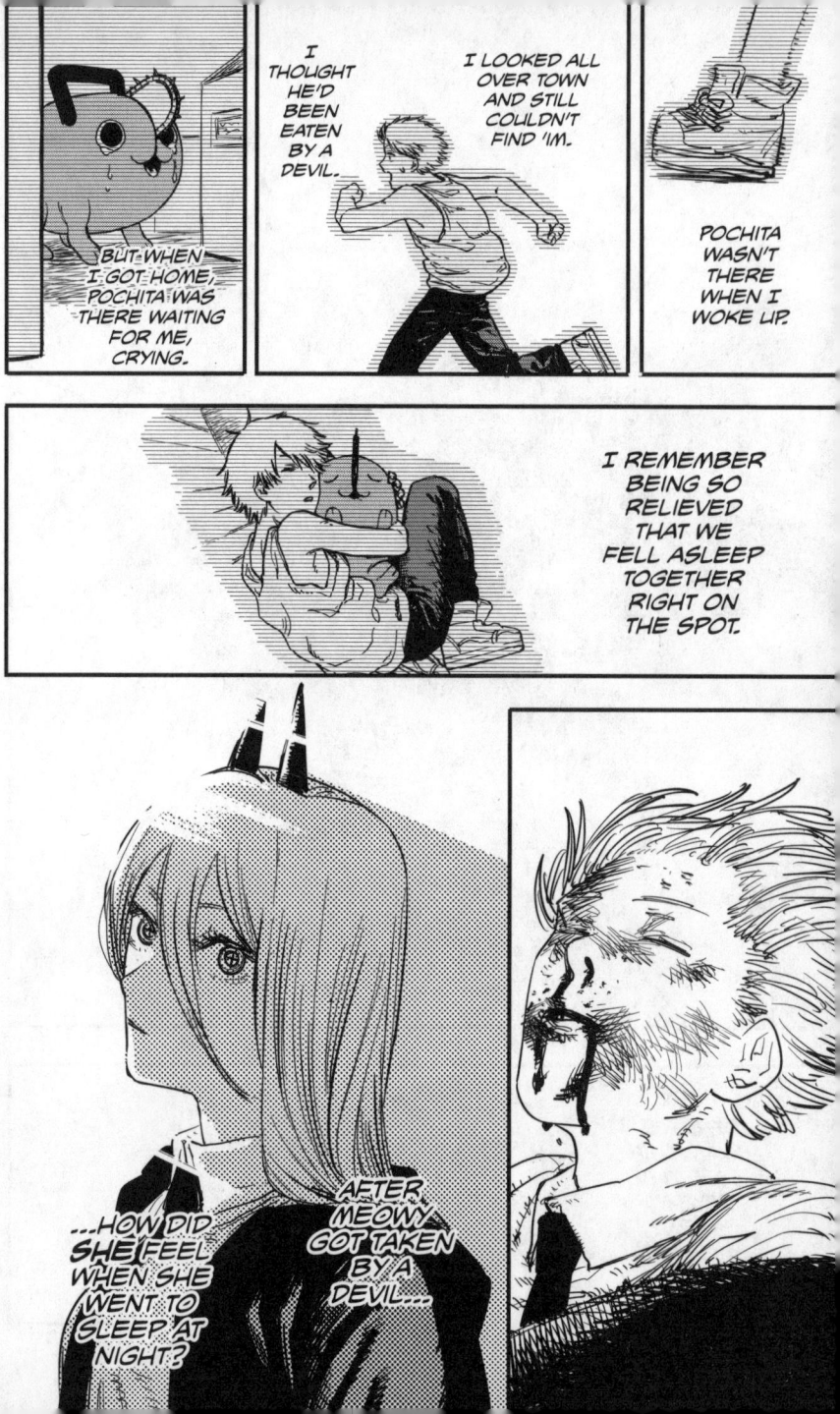
BUT WHEN I GOT HOME, POCHITA WAS THERE WAITING FOR ME, CRYING.
I THOUGHT HE'D BEEN EATEN BY A DEVIL.
I LOOKED ALL OVER TOWN AND STILL COULDN'T FIND 'IM.
POCHITA WASN'T THERE WHEN I WOKE UP.
I REMEMBER BEING SO RELIEVED THAT WE FELL ASLEEP TOGETHER RIGHT ON THE SPOT.
...HOW DID SHE FEEL WHEN SHE WENT TO SLEEP AT NIGHT?
AFTER MEOWY GOT TAKEN BY A DEVIL...

SNAP
SNAP
KRAK
THERE WAS THIS ONE TIME POCHITA WENT MISSING.

GIMME BACK MY BOOBS!
YOU'RE DRINKING MY BLOOD...?! HOW VILE!
I DO NOT HAVE ANY DESIRE TO DRINK *YOUR* BLOOD!

AFTER I'VE GARGLED, I'LL HAVE A VIRGIN AS AN APPETIZER.
FOR THE SOUP, A HEALTHY WOMAN OF RIPE AGE.
THE MAIN COURSE WILL BE A GOOD, PLUMP MAN.
AND FOR DESSERT, I DESIRE A PREGNANT WOMAN!
HRRN ?

AP
FW
KRA
SH
GAAH! MY MOUTH TASTES REVOLTING!
I MUST RINSE IT OUT WITH THE BLOOD OF CHILDREN!

NOTHING BUT DISGUSTING BLOOD! GRRNGH!
DIS-GUST-ING!
gu
IP

GSH
'TIS AN AWFUL FEELING, ISN'T IT?
I KNOW HOW YOU FEEL.

gulp
YOU SAID YOU CAN'T PET POCHITA ANYMORE...

Meee-w!
I NEED BLOOD...
BRING ME A HUMAN IF YOU WANT THE CAT TO LIVE...

I'VE ALWAYS KILLED EVERYTHING THAT MET MY GAZE...
IT FEELS STRANGE TO HEAR A VOICE THAT ISN'T SCREAM-ING...
BLOOD DEVIL!
SO STRANGE ...

lick

spssh

HURRY AND GROW BIG!
I'M EAGER TO KILL YOU!

Meooooow.

FOR A CAT, YOU SMELL TASTY!
MEOWY!
YOUR NAME SHALL BE MEOWY!
METHINKS I'LL FATTEN YOU UP A LITTLE BEFORE I EAT YOU!
YOU'RE ALL SKIN AND BONES...
Mrow!

MROW!
MEOWY...

MEOWY!!
Myah! Myah!
BUT I STILL HAVEN'T PUNISHED YOU FOR BRINGING ME DISGUSTING BLOOD, HAVE I?
Mroow!

BAT DEVIL !!
I BROUGHT YOU A HUMAN AS PROMISED!
NOW GIVE MEOWY BACK!
HRRM ?
AH, YES... WAS THAT THE DEAL?

Chapter 7: Meowy's Whereabouts

chainsaw man

WHAT DO YOU WANT? TO BE FRIENDS WITH DEVILS?
I CAN'T BELIEVE YOU TOOK MY STORY FOR TRUTH.
HUMANS REALLY ARE FOOLISH.

WHAT A REVOLTING TASTE!!
I'LL HAVE TO EAT OTHER HUMANS TO GET RID OF THIS TASTE!
THUMP

NOW I'VE GONE AND REGEN-ERATED ...
...FROM DISGUSTING BLOOD BECAUSE OF YOUUU!!
KRA
KRA

GYAAAAAAAAH!!
GRUSH
HRN?! YOU TASTE DISGUST-ING!!
LAT
JP

GAH!
THIS INFERNAL WOUND FORCED ME TO HIDE MY GRAND SELF!
LOOK AT MY ARM, HUMAN! YOU DAMN HUMANS DID THIS TO ME!
LIKE I CARE, IDIOT!
...SO I'LL HEAL IT WITH HUMAN BLOOD!
HUMANS CARVED THIS WOUND UPON ME...
MY MEAL BARKS!

BAT...
I BROUGHT YOU A HUMAN, JUST AS YOU WISHED!
A YOUNG MALE, EH...? LOOKS LIKE I'LL GET TO DRINK BLOOD BRIMMING WITH LIFE FORCE!
MY FIRST MEAL IN SO LONG!

HE'S A FOOL, BUT HE HAD GOOD INTUITION...
UGH!
UHN...
SL
AM
I HAD TO WAIT THAT LONG TILL I COULD FINALLY GET OUTSIDE TOO!
DON'T COM-PLAIN!
I THOUGHT YOU'D RUN AWAY...
YOU MADE ME WAIT FOR QUITE SOME TIME, BLOOD DEVIL...

WHAM
AH!

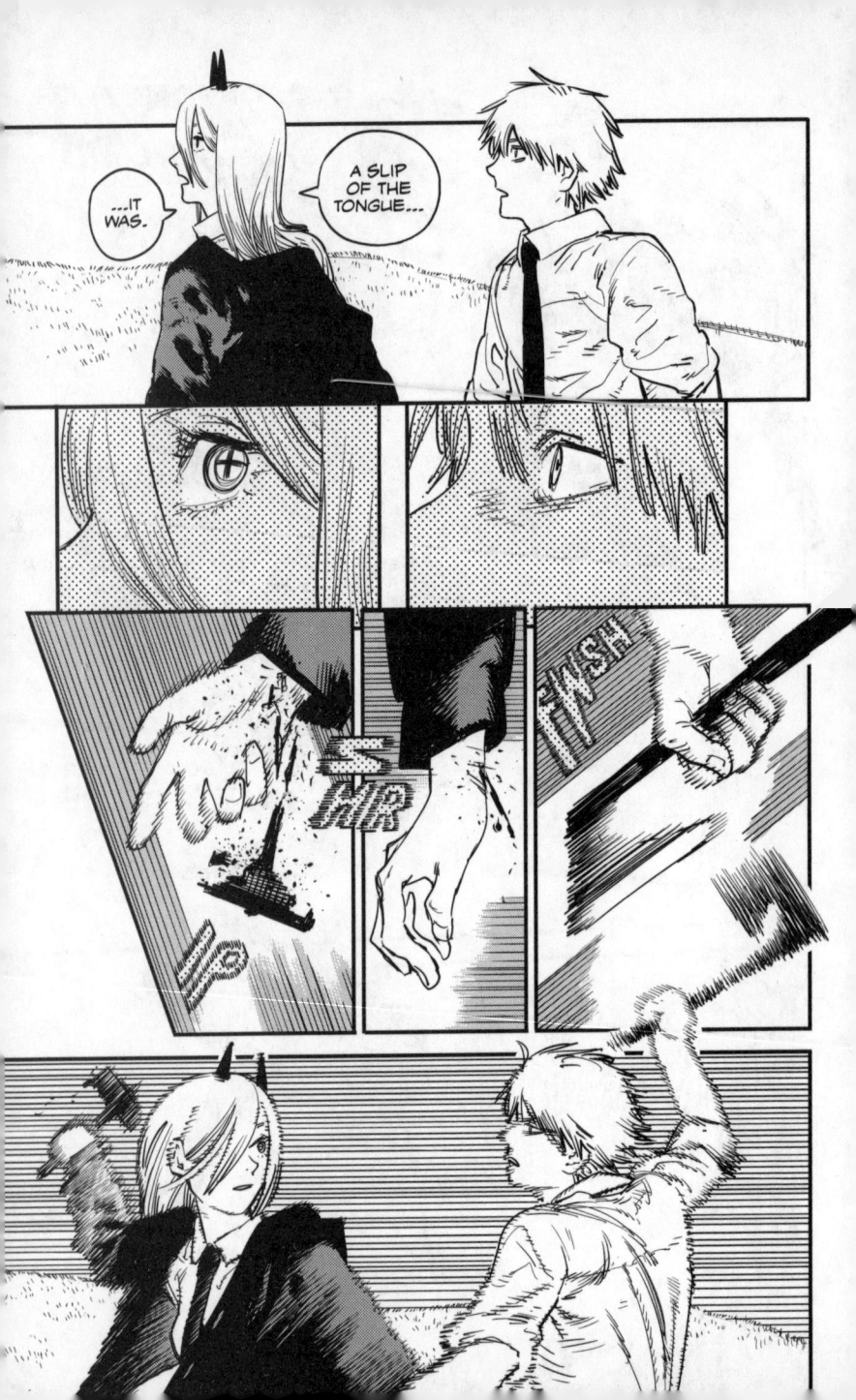
...IT WAS.
A SLIP OF THE TONGUE...
SMR
TWSH

HUMAN JESTS ARE SO UNAMUS-ING!
HUH?
YEAH? WHAT IS IT?
ISN'T IT GONNA USE YOUR CAT AS A HOSTAGE IF YOU SHOW UP?
YOU CAN'T COME THIS CLOSE WITH ME, RIGHT?
OHH? WAS THAT MY STORY?
STORY?

'TIS THAT HOUSE!
MEOWY AND THE DEVIL ARE IN THERE!
HUUUH... THEN LET'S GET OUR BUTTS OVER THERE.
YEAH, I CAN TURN INTO CHAINSAWS!
OHH? GO CHAIN-SAWS?
MAN, I DON'T REALLY WANNA GO ALL CHAINSAWS ON IT CUZ I'LL GET FAINT...

I REALLY DO THINK THAT'S INTEREST-ING.
IT'S INTERESTING AND NOTHING MORE. HE'S USE-LESS.
ONLY PEOPLE WITH GOALS OR CONVICTION SERVE IN PUBLIC SAFETY.
BUT HIM, HE SAID ALL HE WANTS IS TO LIVE THE EASY LIFE.
HE ISN'T FIT FOR PUBLIC SAFETY.
NOT TO MENTION HE THINKS YOU CAN BECOME FRIENDS WITH DEVILS.
HE'S STILL A BRAT.
JUST SOME BRAT.

THE MORE THAT NAME IS FEARED, THE MORE POWERFUL THE DEVIL ITSELF.
BUT WHAT IF THERE WAS A CAR DEVIL? THAT CONJURES UP THE MENTAL IMAGE OF GETTING RUN OVER AND DYING, SO THAT MIGHT BE STRONG.
COFFEE HAS NO SCARY MENTAL IMAGE WHATSOEVER. IF THERE WAS A COFFEE DEVIL, IT WOULD PROBABLY BE WEAK.
DENJI CAN TURN INTO THE CHAINSAW DEVIL.

SL
AM

ALL DEVILS ARE BORN WITH A NAME.

WHY DO YOU HAVE SUCH HIGH HOPES FOR HIM?
DENJI IS DISGUSTING. THERE'S NOTHING INTERESTING ABOUT HIM.

MAKIMA... ARE THE DOGS IN THE SQUAD WE GAVE YOU COMING ALONG...?
WE CAN ONLY PRAY THAT THE DEVILS REMAIN JAPAN'S ONLY ENEMIES.

I HAVE ONE DOG THAT'S PROMIS-ING...
...AND ONE THAT'S INTER-ESTING.

ta
P

A PUPPY I RECENTLY TOOK IN.

INTER-ESTING ...?

BE SURE NOT TO GET ATTACHED.
YOUR JOB IS TO TRAIN DOGS AND USE THEM.

THE SOVIET WAR HAWKS ARE GETTING LOUDER OVER THE AMERICAN MATTER.
WE'RE ALSO HEARING RUMORS THAT THEY'RE USING DEVILS FOR MILITARY PURPOSES.

Chapter 6: Service

CUZ HE'S ALIVE INSIDE ME, RIGHT IN HERE!
I CAN'T EVER PET HIM AGAIN, BUT IT'S OKAY.
HUMANS ARE SO FOOLISH!

I HAD A PET TOO. THIS DEVIL NAMED POCHITA.

THAT MEANS POCHITA DIED, DOES IT NOT?
THE DEAD HAVE NO LIFE!
"THEY'RE IN MY HEART" OR WHATEVER— THAT'S PATHETIC CONSOLATION!

SAY WHAT?

YOU CAN'T EVEN GO OUT ON YOUR OWN?
NOPE. I WAS SO BORED BEING IN HERE ALL THE TIME.
YOUR DAY-LEAVE REQUEST FOR THE FIEND POWER IS APPROVED.
BE BACK BY FIVE O'CLOCK!
Chapter 6: Service
I KNOW WHERE TO FIND THE DEVIL WHO TOOK MEOWY!
THE PROBLEM IS THAT ONLY YOU CAN FIGHT IT.
IF IT SEES ME, IT'LL USE MEOWY AS A SHIELD.
THEN IT WOULD BE CHECK-MATE!

chainsaw man

THAT'S TOTALLY UNFOR-GIVABLE, RIGHT?!
YEAH !!
AS A DEVIL HUNTER, I CAN'T LET 'EM GET AWAY WITH IT!!
YEAH !!
I'LL MURDERIZE THAT DEVIL!!

HOW DARE...
...THEY KIDNAP A POOR CAT!!
OHH?!

THAT DAMN DEVIL!

OHH?

FOR A CAT? THAT'S STUPID!
I'D DO ANYTHING TO TOUCH SOME BOOBS THOUGH.
I DOUBT YOU'D UNDERSTAND SUCH SENTIMENT FOR THE LIKES OF A CAT.
IF I COULD JUST GET MEOWY BACK FROM THAT DEVIL, I'D DO ANYTHING— EVEN ALLY WITH A HUMAN!
...IF YOU GOT MEOWY BACK FROM THAT DEVIL FOR ME?
WHAT IF I SAID I'D LET YOU TOUCH MY CHEST...
HMM ...
OH, BUT IF IT WAS A DOG, I MIGHT GET IT...
SURE ENOUGH, I CAN'T COMPREHEND HUMANS.

I HATE HUMANS!
NOT BECAUSE THEY DID ANYTHING TO ME.
IT'S LIKE A DEVIL INSTINCT. I JUST DO.
I CAN ONLY GET ALONG WITH CATS.
AND I HATE DEVILS TOO.
BECAUSE A DEVIL MADE OFF WITH MY PET, MEOWY!
MAKIMA CAUGHT ME BEFORE I COULD GET MEOWY BACK.
MEOWY MIGHT ALREADY BE DEAD, BUT I CAN'T GIVE UP.

MAYBE THIS ISN'T THE TIME TO BE THINKING ABOUT TOUCHING BOOBS.

Meooow!

STILL, I CAN'T WORK WITH SOME LIAR CHICK...

GETTING TO HAVE SOFT DRINKS IS, LIKE, A DREAM COME TRUE TO ME.
BUT IF WE KEEP SCREWING UP, IT'LL BE WAY WORSE THAN NOT GETTING TO HAVE SOFT DRINKS ANYMORE!

HUH...?!
I-I CAN!

CAN YOU BE QUIET?

GOOD GIRL, POWER.
HONESTLY, I DON'T REALLY CARE WHICH OF YOU WAS AT FAULT.
I WANT TO SEE BIG THINGS FROM YOU TWO.

I'LL SH—! SH-SHOW YOU!

DO YOU THINK YOU CAN SHOW ME THAT?

THIS HUMAN COMMANDED ME TO KILL THE DEVIL!! IT'S TRUE!!
I'M NOT LYING!! HE SAID IT!!
YOU'RE REALLY GONNA LIE AND THROW ME UNDER THE BUS LIKE THAT?!
I NEVER SAID THAT! NOT EVEN CLOSE!
You should be arrested!! You're gonna get arrested for the crime of lying and defamery or whatever!!
Seriously?! Miss Makima, this Devil is a Liar!!
What a creep!
Quit talkin' all weird to sound cooler than you are!!
It's so creepy!!
HUMANS TELL NASTY LIES! I ONLY DID AS I WAS TOLD, 'TIS TRUTH!!
ONLY HUMANS LIE!!
NO!
THIS DECEIVER TOLD ME TO DO IT! DEVILS CAN'T LIE!
That's not a thing!!
You're the proof, stupidface!! You lying liar!!

Exci—?!
POWER, SINCE YOU WERE THE BLOOD DEVIL BEFORE YOU BECAME A FIEND, BATTLING USING BLOOD IS YOUR SPECIALTY...
...BUT YOU'RE SO EXCITABLE... MAYBE YOU WEREN'T CUT OUT TO BE A DEVIL HUNTER?
HUH ?!
THIS GUY SAID TO KILL IT, HE DID!
THISH—

Suda Books
Fried Chicken
IT'S CONSIDERED OBSTRUCTION OF JUSTICE WHEN A PUBLIC SAFETY HUNTER KILLS A DEVIL A CIVILIAN HUNTER IS ALREADY ENGAGED WITH.
NORMALLY, YOU'D GET ARRESTED FOR IT.
REALLY? YOU'RE BLAMING ME TOO?
AND YOU, DENJI, YOU NEED TO KEEP HER UNDER CONTROL.
POWER, YOU NEED TO THINK A LITTLE MORE BEFORE YOU ACT.

—CUMBER
...
GA HA HA HA HA HA!!
I DID IT! THE GLORY IS MINE!!

Nerima
タウンページ
THE SEA—

Nerima Station
THE SCENE IS LOCKED DOWN AND CIVILIANS ARE EVACUATED.
REQUESTING BACKUP AT NERIMA STATION.
IT'S THE SEA CUCUMBER DEVIL.
SEA CUCUMBER DEVIL.
HUH? I SAID...

VPP
HAIR
E GO!

HE TEAMED ME UP WITH POWER TO KEEP ME FROM SHOWING WHAT I GOT.
HE'S TRYING TO FORCE ME OUT!
THAT JERK... HE SET ME UP DIDN'T HE?!
I SMELL BLOOD!!
HEY! WHOA, WHOA, WHOA! WHERE DO YOU THINK YOU'RE GOING?!
FIGHT TIME! FIGHT TIME! BATTLE TIME!
SHE'S FAST!

There aren't any Devils at all!

Then how are we going to deliver results?!
Wait, what?!

The nobody devils all flee from my scent, I'm sure!
Before I became a fiend, I was a greatly feared devil!

Likely because of ME!

He's the one who paired you two up.
If you have any questions, ask Hayakawa.

IF YOU TELL THEM THAT AND SHOW THEM YOUR BADGE, THEY SHOULD SCOWL AND LEAVE YOU ALONE.
AS I'VE SAID BEFORE, PUBLIC SAFETY DEVIL EXTERMINATION SPECIAL DIVISION 4 IS AN EXPERIMENTAL SQUAD.
IF IT CAN'T DELIVER RESULTS, THE HIGHER-UPS MIGHT BREAK IT UP AT ANY TIME.
YOU TWO KNOW WHAT WILL HAPPEN TO YOU THEN, RIGHT?

BUT POWER HAS HIGH MENTAL FACULTIES, SO I PUT HER IN HAYAKAWA'S SQUAD.
FIENDS ARE TARGETS FOR EXTERMINATION, SAME AS DEVILS.
HER HORNS WILL ATTRACT ATTENTION, SO ONLY PATROL PLACES WITH LITTLE TRAFFIC.
We're with Public Safety Devil Extermination Special Division 4, sirrrs.
IF YOU RUN INTO ANY CIVILIAN DEVIL HUNTERS, OR GET QUESTIONED BY THE POLICE...

HUMAN! HURRY UP AND LET ME KILL SOMETHING!
I THIRST FOR BLOOD!

I CAN FORGIVE SOME CRAZINESS AS LONG AS SHE'S PRETTY...
THE ISSUE IS HOW I'M GONNA TOUCH THOSE BOOBS...

Chapter 5:
A Way to Touch Some Boobs

Chainsaw man

WAIT, YOU'RE A FIEND?!
YOUR NAME IS POWER ?!
POWER?!
FIENDS CAN BE DEVIL HUNTERS ?!
WeLL, WHAT-EVER!!
Lookin' forward TO WORKIN' WITH ya!

HEY, HEY, HEY!
GROVEL, HUMAN!!
MY NAME IS POWER!
ARE YOU MY BUDDY OR WHATEVER?!

A BUDDY ...?
I'M PAIRING YOU UP WITH A BUDDY STARTING TODAY.
MAKIMA SAID SHE LIKED ME... BUT...
...IF I ASK TO TOUCH HER CHEST, THERE'S A CHANCE SHE'LL HATE ME...
IN PUBLIC SAFETY, FOR SMALL-SCALE MISSIONS, PATROLLING AND SO ON, WE ACT IN PAIRS FOR SAFETY'S SAKE.
PERFECT TIMING— LOOKS LIKE YOUR BUDDY'S HERE.
BE CARE-FUL...
SHE'S A FIEND.

FRUIT?
MELONS !!

TO WHAT, NOW...?

HEY! PAY ATTENTION, YOU IDIOT!

JUMPING STRAIGHT TO SLEEPING WITH A WOMAN WOULD BE TOUGH FOR ME...
BUT IF IT'S BOOBS ...
IF IT'S BOOBS, IF I'VE GOT A STRONG WILL AND INITIATIVE, COULDN'T I TOUCH THEM...?
I GAVE UP ON IT FOREVER AGO CUZ I THOUGHT IT WAS IMPOSSIBLE FOR ME...
BUT I HAVE A DECENT JOB NOW. COULDN'T I DO IT?
SO THAT'S WHAT HE MEANT! I'VE FOUND IT, DUDE...
WHAT I'M SERIOUS ABOUT!
MY GOAL!
IT'S...!
EVERYONE IS SERIOUS ABOUT THIS BUT YOU.

I WANNA TOUCH SOME BOOBS...

WITH A PRETTY GIRL CLOSE BY...
I GET TO BATHE EVERY DAY.
AND EAT GOOD FOOD.
FOR THE GUYS BELOW, IT'S PROTECTING THEIR FAMILIES.
I BET HIS ULTIMATE GOAL IS A REVENGE THING.
I HAVE A FULL LIFE NOW... BUT IT DOES KINDA FEEL LIKE SOMETHING'S MISSING.
WAS THERE SOMETHING ELSE? MY REAL, TRUE GOAL...?
DOES MAKIMA HAVE ONE TOO?
DOES MAKIMA ALSO...

SHOW ME YOUR DREAMS.
HE'S STILL CHASING HIS.
IT'S JUST THAT I'VE ALREADY CROSSED THE FINISH LINE TO MY DREAM.
I'M LIVING A DREAM LIFE, JUST LIKE IN OUR CONTRACT, AREN'T I?
I'M SERIOUS ABOUT THIS TOO, POCHITA.

BLAAAH... HE SURE HAS A SHORT TEMPER...
THE TRUTH IS, I JUST DIDN'T WANNA GET BLOOD ON THESE DIRTY MAGAZINES...
ALL RIGHT! Sexiness confirmed!
CUZ WITH THE CHAINSAWS, BLOOD ENDS UP SPRAYING ALL OVER.
I DID YOU A FAVOR KILLING YOU QUICK, SO I'M TAKING THESE!
flip

EVERYONE IS SERIOUS ABOUT THIS BUT YOU.
WHAT DO YOU WANT? TO BE FRIENDS WITH THEM?
I WANT TO KILL DEVILS IN WAYS THAT CAUSE THEM TO SUFFER AS MUCH AS POSSIBLE.
CUZ I DON'T HAVE ANY FRIENDS...
IF THERE ARE DEVILS I COULD BE FRIENDS WITH, THEN YEAH, I DO.
I'LL REMEMBER THOSE WORDS...
SLAM

BANG
LISTEN UP. DON'T YOU FORGET THIS.
FIENDS ARE BONA FIDE DEVILS TOO.
A DEVIL HUNTER SHOULDN'T BE SYMPATHIZING WITH DEVILS.

MY ENTIRE FAMILY WAS KILLED BY A DEVIL RIGHT BEFORE MY EYES.

THE COPS DOWN THERE? I'VE GONE DRINKING WITH THEM BEFORE.
THEY'RE RISKING THEIR LIVES TO DO THEIR JOBS, TO PROTECT THEIR WIVES AND KIDS.

HEY.
WHY DIDN'T YOU USE YOUR DEVIL POWER?
OHH, WELL... WHEN I USE MY POWER TO KILL DEVILS...
...IT LOOKS SUPER PAINFUL.
LIKE, UHHH, I COULD'VE ENDED UP AS A FIEND LIKE THIS GUY TOO, RIGHT?
SO I GUESS I WANTED TO GIVE THE POOR GUY...
...A PAINLESS DEATH...

DON'T LOOK! I'LL KILL YOU! I'LL KILL YOU! I'LL KILL YOU DEVIL HUNTERS!

TURN INTO A DEVIL. SHOW ME YOUR POWER.
I'LL DECIDE WHETHER YOU'RE USEFUL OR NOT.
YOU KILL THIS ONE.
FIENDS HAVE THE DEVIL'S PERSONALITY.

gch
ak
THEN AREN'T I ONE?
OHH.
OH REALLY? UH...
NO.
THEIR HEADS HAVE DISTINCT SHAPES.
A DEVIL THAT'S TAKEN OVER A PERSON'S CORPSE...
THAT'S A FIEND.
WH
AM
WELL, YOU'LL UNDERSTAND WHEN YOU SEE ONE.

MR. HAYAKAWA, IS THAT A NEWBIE WITH YOU?
WE'LL LET YOU DEVIL HUNTERS HANDLE THE REST.
THE FIEND TARGET IS HOLED UP IN A ROOM ON THE SECOND FLOOR.

WHAT? DIDN'T YOU LEARN ANYTHING IN SCHOOL?
NOPE, DIDN'T GO TO SCHOOL.

HEY, WHAT'S A FIEND?

PAID DAYS OFF, HUH-HUMM HUH-HUMM-HUM HUH-HUMM HUH-HUMMM HUM!
UNION JOB, HUMM HUH-HUMM HUH HUH HUH HUH-HUMMM!
YOU'RE TAKING TOO LONG IN THE BATH!
bam
bam
bam
DON'T SLEEP ON THE TOILET!
WE'VE GOT A FIEND INSIDE AN EAST NERIMA RESIDENCE.
CIVILIAN EVACUATION AND LOCKDOWN OF THE SCENE IS COMPLETE AT THIS TIME.

TA-DAA
AND THE ULTIMATE BREAD IS READY!

STRAWBERRY JAM, PLUM JAM, MARMALADE AAAND...

...BUTTER AND HONEYYY AND... SHAKE SOME CINNAMON ON THERE TOO.

Mm!

Chapter 4: Power

Chain

saw

man

I WANNA HUG HER AGAIN.
Say WHAT?!

THEN IS SHE A GOOD PERSON?
WE'RE DEVIL HUNTERS, REMEMBER?
IF YOU'RE A DEVIL, JUST BE GRATEFUL WE'RE LETTING YOU LIVE.
IF YOU THINK SO, THEN GIVE UP ON HER.
OF COURSE SHE'S A GOOD PERSON...
I OWE HER MY LIFE...

本ビル
タツキバンク
FYI, THEY TOLD ME I CAN KILL YOU IF YOU RUN AWAY.
TURNS OUT YOU'RE GONNA LIVE WITH ME SO WE CAN KEEP AN EYE ON YOU.
IS MAKIMA A BAD PERSON?
HEY...

IF DENJI EVER QUITS OR DISOBEYS ORDERS...
...HE'LL BE PUT DOWN AS A DEVIL.

IT MEANS WE'LL BE WORKING TOGETHER UNTIL DEATH DO US PART.

WAIT... WHAT'S THAT MEAN?

JUST WHO IS THIS GUY?
ソダワ

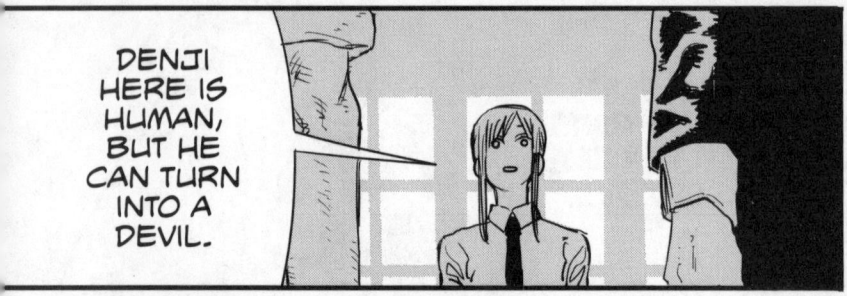
DENJI HERE IS HUMAN, BUT HE CAN TURN INTO A DEVIL.

ARE YOU SERIOUS?
I'VE ONLY HEARD FLIMSY RUMORS ABOUT CASES LIKE THAT...

HOW DO YOU LIKE THAT?! BADASS, RIGHT?!

DENJI IS SPECIAL.
SO IT'S BEEN DECIDED THAT WE'LL TREAT HIM AS A SPECIAL CASE.

I'M GLAD YOU GUYS ARE HITTING IT OFF.

THIS THUG?! REALLY ?!
Squad?

I'M PUTTING DENJI IN YOUR SQUAD, HAYAKAWA.

BUT WE ALREADY HAVE SO MANY TROUBLE-MAKERS AS IT IS!
IF WE ADD ANY MORE WEIRDOS...

THAT I'D TRY OPERATING IT WITH A UNIQUE EXPERIMENTAL SETUP.
I TOLD YOU WHEN WE CREATED YOUR SQUAD, DIDN'T I?

A TESTICLE DEVIL ATTACKED HIS BALLS.

THAT'S A LIE... HE MADE THAT UP...

CAN YOU GET ALONG?
SO WHAT DO YOU THINK?
HMMM.

THIS GUY IS SCUM...
NOT A CHANCE.

YOU JUST WANT HER FOR YOUR-SELF!!
HUH?! WHAT GIVES ?!
...HAS NO PLACE LIKING MAKIMA!
A THUG LIKE YOU...

CRAP.

THUD

YOU... SERI-OUSLY ...

...ONLY AIM FOR...
...THE BALLS...

MY LIFE ISN'T MINE ALONE.
ACTUALLY, I TAKE THAT BACK.
GFF!
DO
NG

MAYBE I BECAME A DEVIL HUNTER FOR A REALLY SHALLOW REASON...

...BUT I'M WILLING TO *DIE* TO KEEP LIVING LIKE THIS.

YOU SURE ARE A NICE GUY...
WHAK
WHAK
WHAK
THE CROTCH!
AIM FOR!
ONLY!
WHAK
WHAK
WHAK
WHAK
WHAK
WHEN I!
GUYS!
I!
FIGHT!
huff huff
WHEW!
AND A HOT DOG TOO...
TODAY, I ATE UDON FOR THE FIRST TIME...

DO
NG
WHUMP

ptoo
sn
at
...YOU GOT SCARED OF A DEVIL AND RAN AWAY.
I'LL DO YOU A FAVOR AND TELL MAKIMA...

MAYBE MY KINDNESS ISN'T GETTING THROUGH TO YOU...
WHAT'S YOUR PROB-LEM...?

THE ONLY ONES STILL ALIVE ARE THOSE WHO HAVE STRONG CONVICTION.
AMONG MY PEERS, THE ONES WHO BECAME DEVIL HUNTERS JUST FOR THE MONEY GOT KILLED BY DEVILS. ALL OF THEM.
THE PEOPLE WHO GO INTO THIS JOB FOR SHALLOW REASONS END UP DEAD, KID.

DING diiING.

THEN I WAS RIGHT TO BEAT YOU UP.

LEMME GUESS. YOU BECAME A DEVIL HUNTER CUZ YOU'VE GOT YOUR EYE ON MAKIMA?

CRACK
SHATTER
YOU SHOULD QUIT.
IF YOU SHOW UP TOMORROW, I'LL GIVE YOU ANOTHER THRASHING.

DOES MAKIMA HAVE A BOY-FRIEND?
HEY, SIR.
HEY, TELL ME.
C'MERE.
HEY!

IF YOU PERFORM WELL, WE'LL BE ABLE TO WORK TOGETHER.
SO KEEP YOUR CHIN UP, OKAY?

FOR TODAY, TAG ALONG WITH HIM.
THIS IS AKI HAYA-KAWA.
HE'S THREE YEARS YOUR SENIOR HERE.
I'M NOT WORKING WITH YOU, MISS MAKIMA?
OF COURSE NOT.
Nooo! Miss Maki-maaa!!
YOU AND MISS MAKIMA ARE IN COMPLETELY DIFFERENT LEAGUES.
WE'RE GOING ON PATROL.

ONCE YOU'RE CHANGED, I'LL INTRODUCE YOU TO ONE OF YOUR COLLEAGUES.

YES ?!
DENJI.

WE TYPICALLY WORK IN UNIFORM. PUT THIS ON.

WE PUBLIC SAFETY DEVIL HUNTERS...
...GET A LOT OF PAID DAYS OFF AND THE BEST BENEFITS PACKAGE.
INCLUDING CIVILIANS, THERE ARE MORE THAN A THOUSAND DEVIL HUNTERS IN TOKYO.
IF MAKIMA LIKES ME, THEN...
I WANNA DO IT!! I WANNA DO THAT STUFF SO BAD!!
AND IF WE'RE IN THAT KINDA RELATIONSHIP, COULDN'T WE DO THAT KINDA STUFF TOO...?
...AS WE WORK TOGETHER, WON'T WE END UP BECOMING, YOU KNOW...?

Chapter 3:
Arrival in Tokyo
THIS IS DEVIL HUNTER TOKYO HQ.

Chapter 3: Arrival in Tokyo

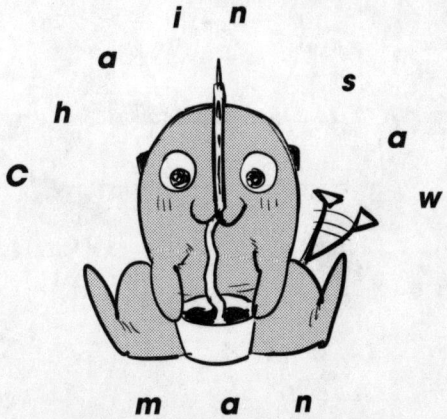
i n
a
s
h
a
c
w
m a n

SOMEONE LIKE THIS BOY NAMED DENJI.
DENJI ...?
WAIT, THAT'S ME...

MAKIMA.
HEY, UH!
WHAT'S YOUR NAME...?
WHAT TYPE OF GUY DO YOU LIKE?
MISS MAKIMA ...
W...
HMMM...

"Ah-h."
Say
Ahh.
GOOD?
Woof!
YOU REALLY ARE LIKE A DOG.
HARD TO BELIEVE YOU ACTUALLY ENJOYED THAT SOGGY UDON...
WHAT A GOOD BOY.

OKAY...

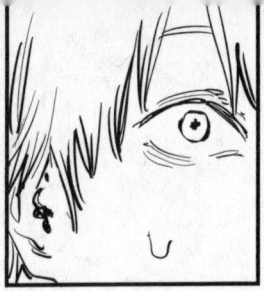

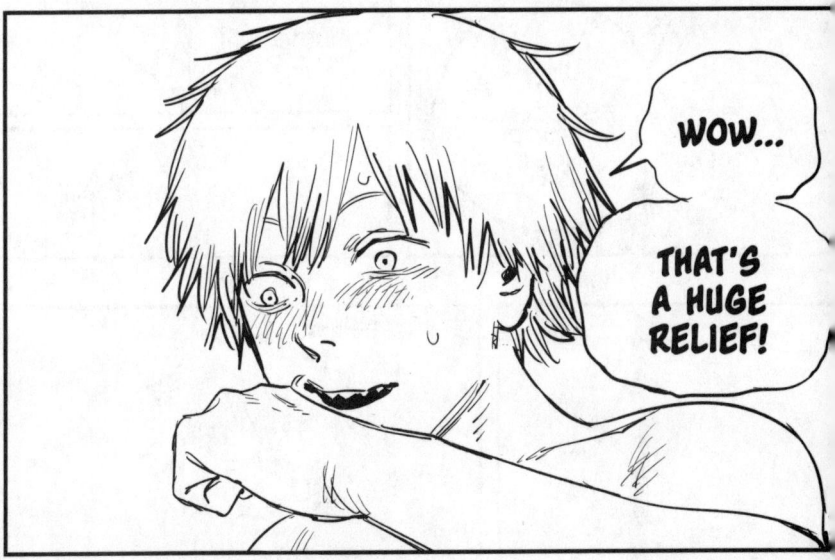
WOW...
THAT'S A HUGE RELIEF!

I CA—
I can't.

I'LL EAT THAT UDON ...
CAN YOU FEED YOUR-SELF?
YOU LOOK UNSTEADY.

gurgle

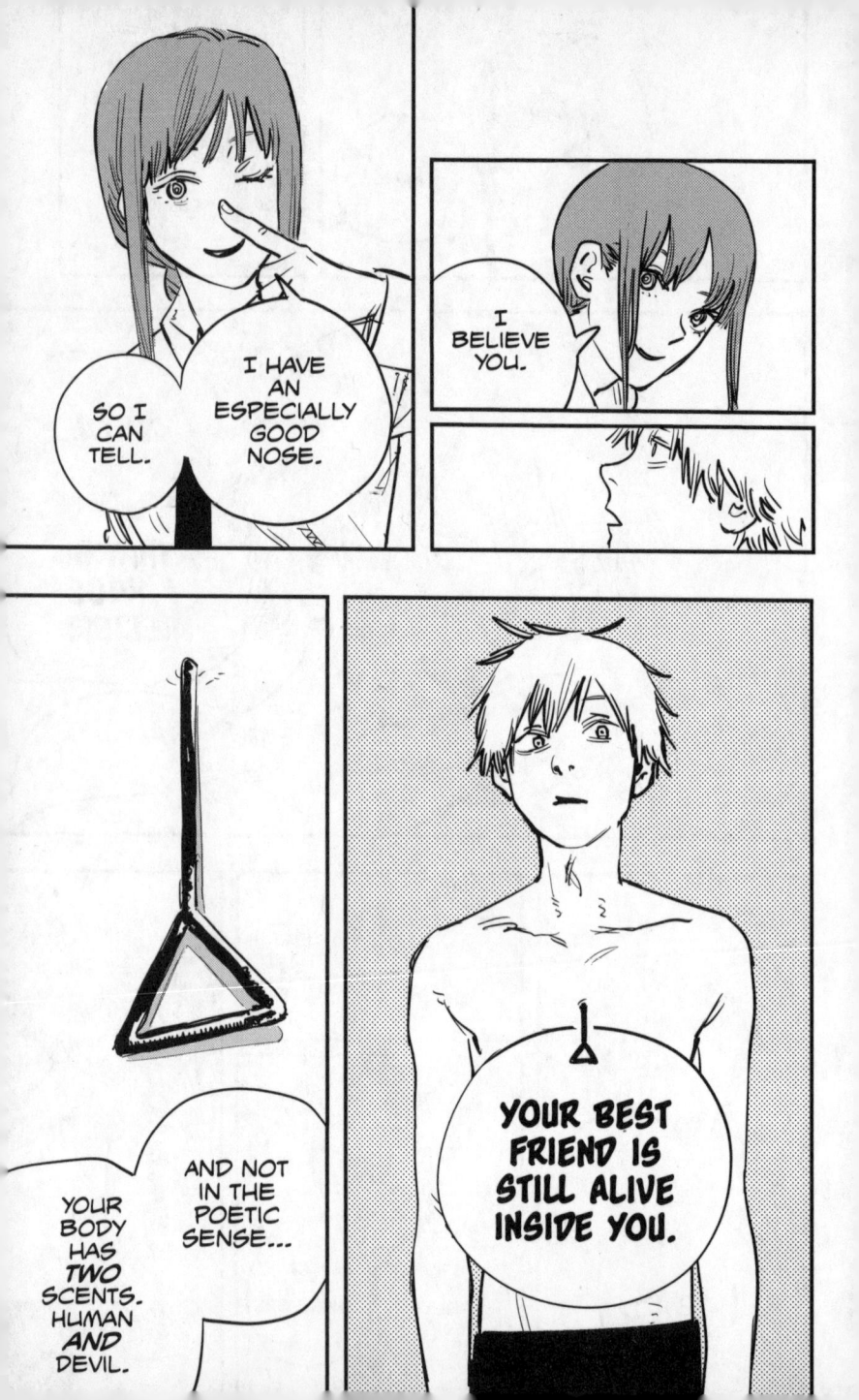
I HAVE AN ESPECIALLY GOOD NOSE.
SO I CAN TELL.
I BELIEVE YOU.
YOUR BODY HAS TWO SCENTS. HUMAN AND DEVIL.
AND NOT IN THE POETIC SENSE...
YOUR BEST FRIEND IS STILL ALIVE INSIDE YOU.

HOW DID YOUR BODY END UP LIKE THAT?
MY PET DEVIL BECAME MY HEART.
UNBELIEVABLE, RIGHT?
THAT POCHITA DIED FOR ME...
I DON'T WANNA BELIEVE IT EITHER.
HISTORICALLY SPEAKING, YOUR CONDITION HAS VERY FEW PRECEDENTS.
SO FEW IT HASN'T EVEN BEEN NAMED.

topple
UH-OH.
WHUMP
YOU OKAY?
SHE SMELLS GOOD...
SORRY... I END UP CUTTING MY OWN BODY WITH THE CHAINSAWS TOO...
LOOKS LIKE I LOSE TOO MUCH BLOOD AND GET FAINT...

I SEE YOU'RE A USEFUL DOG.
WOOF...

VRRR
SHH

EE!
WHAT A RELIEF. I WON'T FEEL BAD...
...FOR KILLING A LOWLIFE LIKE YOU.
OW OW OW OW OW OW OW OW?!

I'M GONNA HAVE SOME FUN WITH THIS FEMALE BRAT NOW.
BEHAVE YOURSELF OVER THERE, 'KAY?
ARRGH!!
I CAN CONTROL ANY MUSCLES I'M TOUCHING!
twitch
AH HA HA HA HA HA!
HEH HEH HEH...
AH HA HA HA HA HA HA!
twitch
twitch
twitch
twitch
twitch

HAH! I WIN!
HA HA HA!
I'LL SHOW YOU SOMETHING COOL BEFORE YOU DIE.
I'M THE MUSCLE DEVIL, AND THAT MEANS...
WHAT THE HELL IS THIS?!

clasp
Ah ha ha ha ha!
AH HA!
CAN WE...?
WE TOTALLY CAN!
AH HA HA HA HA HA HA HA!
HA HA HA...
HA HA... HUH?
AH HA HA HA HA HA HA HA HA!

I WAS BUDDIES WITH A DEVIL TOO. I KNOW...
...THERE ARE GOOD DEVILS.
HUH?
HEY... WANNA RUN AWAY TOGETHER? THE THREE OF US...?
SO DO YOU WANNA RUN AWAY...?
BUT IF I LET THIS DEVIL GO, THEY'RE GONNA KILL ME.

WHEN HE WAS HITTING ME IN THE PARKING LOT TODAY...
...THIS NICE DEVIL SAVED ME!
MY DADDY... WHEN HE HAS A BAD DAY, HE BEATS ME.
SO, PLEASE! DON'T KILL HIM...
OUR USELESS DOGS GET EUTHANIZED.

AH.
WAIT, WHAT?
OH, PLEASE! LET THIS DEVIL GO!

I JUST REMEMBERED POCHITA'S DEAD...
BLAAAH...
Na na na!
Ah na na na!

TREATIN' ME LIKE A DAMN DOG...!
I EVEN LIKED HER A LITTLE.
I THOUGHT SHE WAS NICE.
I CAN'T BELIEVE SHE WAS THAT SCARY!
Woof!

...OUR USELESS DOGS GET EUTHANIZED.
I HEARD FROM AN ACQUAINTANCE IN THE CRIME SCENE DIVISION THAT...

YES'M.

WHAT'S YOUR ANSWER?

COME ON! THE UDON'LL GET SOGGY. OFF YOU GO!

HUH?! UH, BUT I'M HAVING UDON TOO.

OKAY, DENJI...
I DON'T WANT MY NOODLES TO GET SOGGY. YOU GO KILL THE DEVIL BY YOURSELF.

REALLY?
PLEASE REMAIN INSIDE THE BUILDING FOR YOUR SAFETY.
AN EXPERIENCED DEVIL HUNTER IS ON THE JOB, SIR. HE'LL SAVE YOUR DAUGHTER.

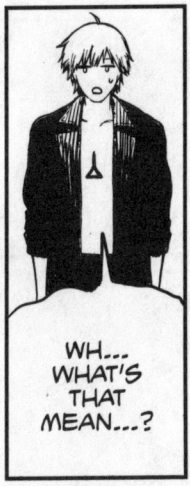
WH... WHAT'S THAT MEAN...?

DID YOU FORGET? YOU'RE MY PET.
ONLY ANSWER WITH "YES" OR "WOOF."

I DON'T NEED A DOG WHO SAYS "NO."

A D-DEVIL SNATCHED MY DAUGHTER!
MY LITTLE GIRL, IT—
WHAT HAP-PENED?
I'M A PUBLIC SAFETY DEVIL HUNTER, SIR.
IT TOOK HER INTO THE WOODS!!
IT'S DENJI!
WHAT'S YOUR NAME?
CURRY UDON'S UP!
OH... THAT'S ME.

SURE THING.
...A HOT DOG! IS THAT OKAY?!
OH, I'LL HAVE UDON AND... UDON AND...
H—
H-HELP ME!

ALSO, YOU'LL DRAW ATTENTION SHIRTLESS. PUT THIS ON.
AND BY A PRETTY GIRL, AT THAT...
THIS'S THE FIRST TIME I'VE BEEN TREATED NICE.
PEOPLE ALWAYS CALL ME DIRTY AND SMELLY. NOBODY EVER COMES NEAR ME.
I'M IN LOVE.

gurrrrgle

SORRY, UH... I'M BROKE...

THAT'S MY STOMACH...

LET'S GRAB SOME FOOD AT A REST STOP.
WE HAVEN'T HAD BREAKFAST EITHER.

PICK ANYTHING YOU WANT. I'LL PAY.
Really ?!

Chapter 2: The Place Where Pochita Is

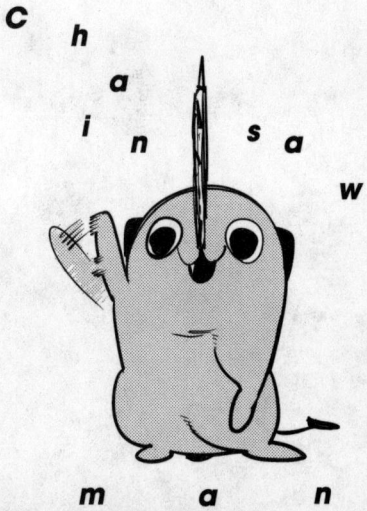
C h a i n s a w
m a n

LET'S SEE...
BREAD WITH BUTTER AND JAM...
SALAD, COFFEE...
AND... MAYBE DESSERT?

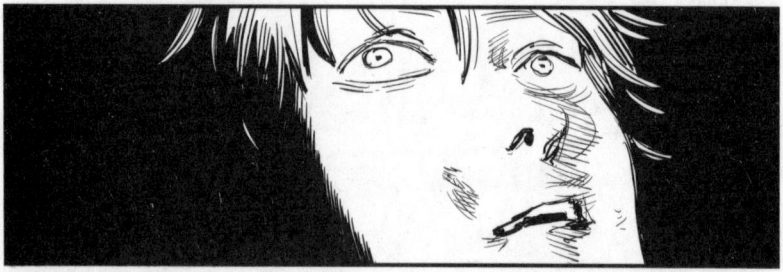

THAT'S A DREAM COME TRUE...

I CAME HERE TO KILL THE ZOMBIE DEVIL.
I'M A PUBLIC SAFETY DEVIL HUNTER.

YOU HAVE TWO CHOICES.
ONE, BE KILLED BY ME AS A DEVIL.
OR TWO, BE KEPT BY ME AS A HUMAN.

FOOD...?
WHAT WOULD I GET FOR BREAK-FAST?

IF YOU'RE MY PET, I'LL GIVE YOU FOOD.

YOU'RE HUMAN...
ANY CHANCE IT'S A DEVIL POSSES-SION?
NONE. YOU CAN SEE POSSESSION ON THEIR FACES.

DID YOU DO THIS?

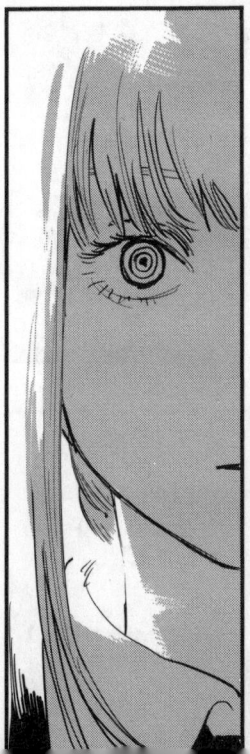

topple
HOLD ME...

H...

GOT A LIVE ONE.
HMM...
YOU HAVE A PECULIAR SMELL.
IT ISN'T HUMAN OR DEVIL.

LOOKS LIKE SOMEONE BEAT US TO THE PUNCH.

GU-A HA HA HA HA-!!

I KNOW!
IF I KILL EVERY LAST ONE OF YOU...
...IT'S BYE-BYE, DEBT!

...I GOTTA KILL DEVILS DEAD!
AND SINCE I GET PAID TO BE A DEVIL HUNTER...

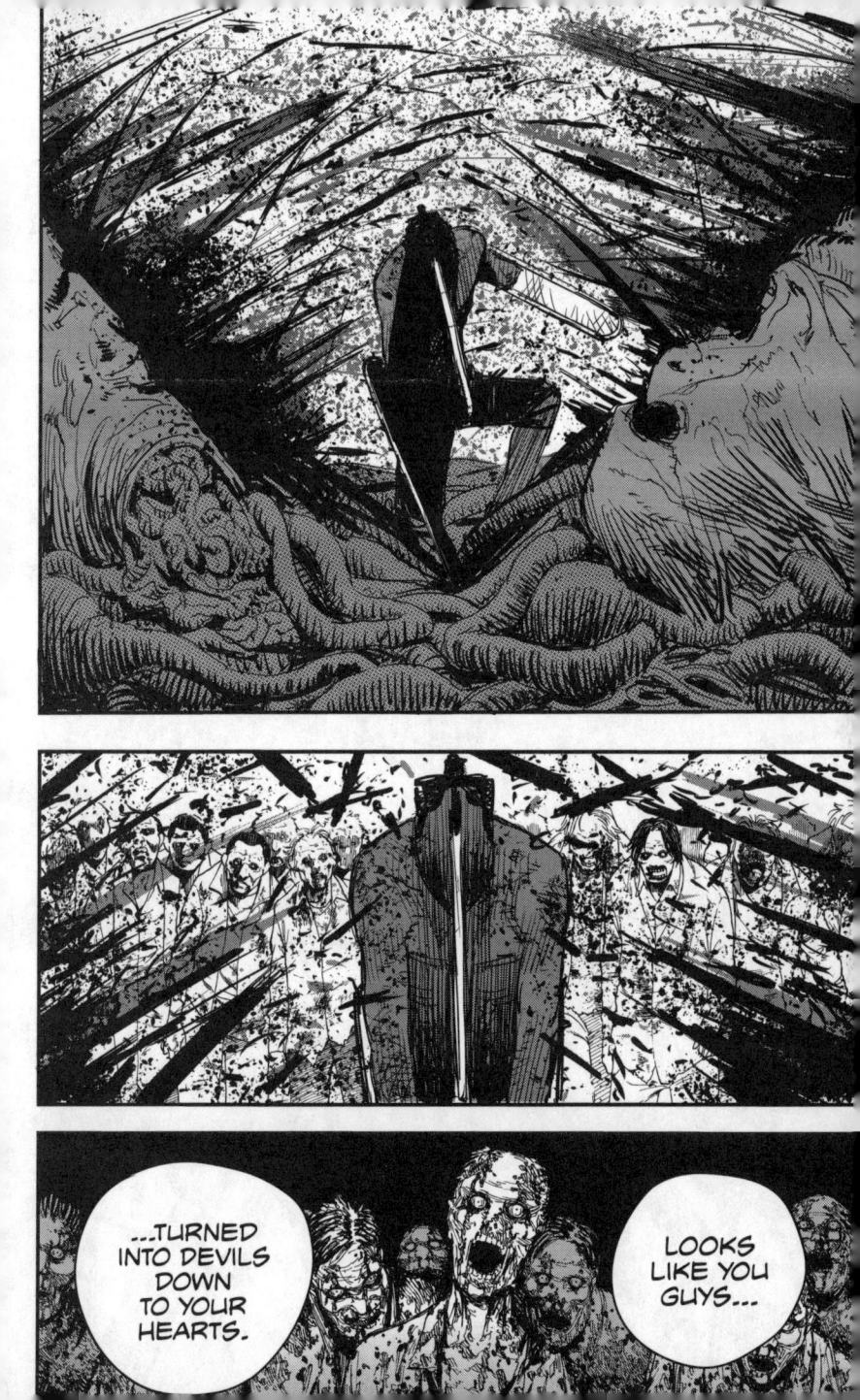
...TURNED INTO DEVILS DOWN TO YOUR HEARTS.
LOOKS LIKE YOU GUYS...

WHAT ARE YOU ...?!
DID THAT SMALL-FRY DEVIL TAKE OVER THE BODY...?!
THEN YOU'RE ONE OF US, RIGHT?!

ZR
HE HAS TO STAY DEAD IF WE EAT HIM...

IF YOU'RE GONNA GET IN OUR WAY...
...THEN DIE!
BROOM

I SHOULDA BEEN HAPPY AS LONG AS I HAD POCHITA.
BUT I STILL DREAMED OF A BETTER LIFE.
MAYBE I'M THE SAME.
HOW COME THEY WANTED AN EVEN BETTER LIFE?
THESE GUYS ALREADY HAD PLENTY.
OH, I GET IT. EVERYBODY DREAMS. YOU CAN'T HELP IT.
THEN DREAMING'S NOT A BAD THING.
IT'S NOT A BAD THING, BUT...

WE CUT HIM TO RIBBONS AND HE'S STILL ALIVE?!
GROSS!
I *REALLY* HATE DEVIL HUNTERS!

HUH?

YOU GUYS!! EAT THAT FREAK!!

POCHITA!

...SHOW ME YOUR DREAMS.

MY WOUNDS ARE GONE...

POCHITA!

I'VE ALWAYS...
...LOVED LISTENING TO YOU TALK ABOUT YOUR DREAMS.

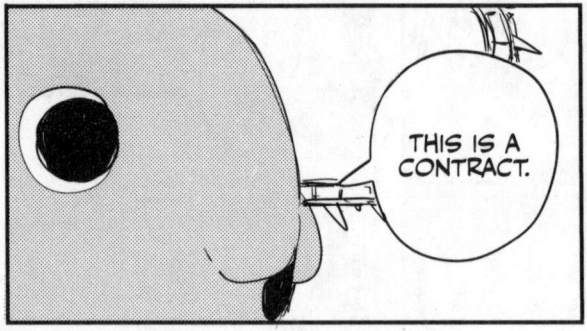
THIS IS A CONTRACT.

I'LL GIVE YOU MY HEART.
IN EXCHANGE ...

Woof !!!

POCHITA ...

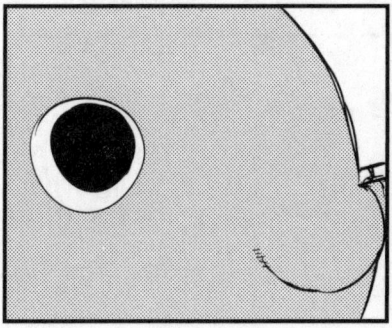

DID YOU TAKE MY BODY? LIKE I TOLD YOU TO?

IF I DO, YOU'LL BE MY ONE REGRET.

YOU COULD STARVE TO DEATH.
OR GET KILLED BY ANOTHER DEVIL HUNTER.

I HEARD SOME DEVILS CAN TAKE OVER DEAD BODIES.

VREEEEE
I MIGHT DIE WHILE I'M FIGHTING DEVILS.
POCHITA ...
THM
P
THO
OM

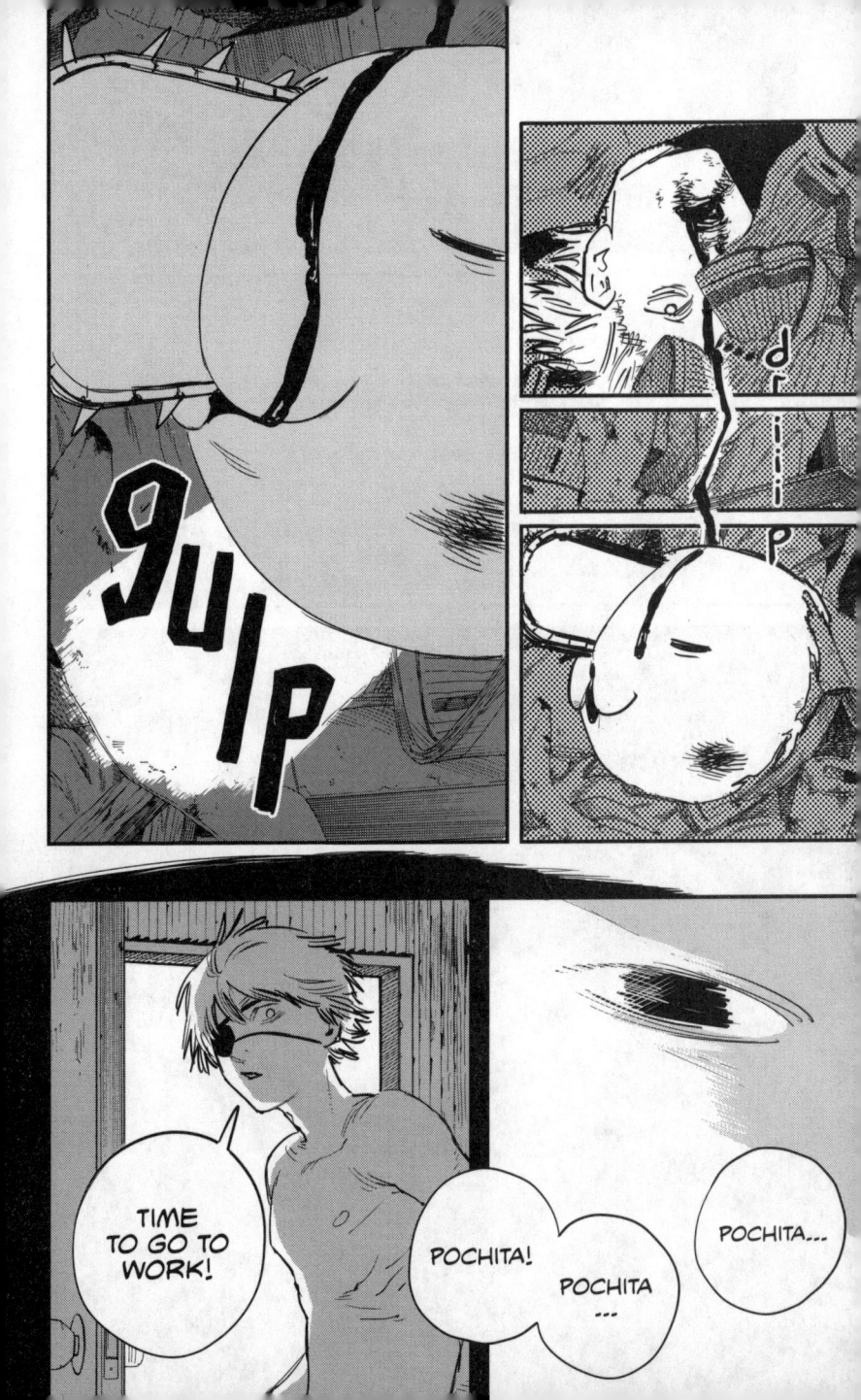
gulp
TIME TO GO TO WORK!
POCHITA!
POCHITA ...
POCHITA...

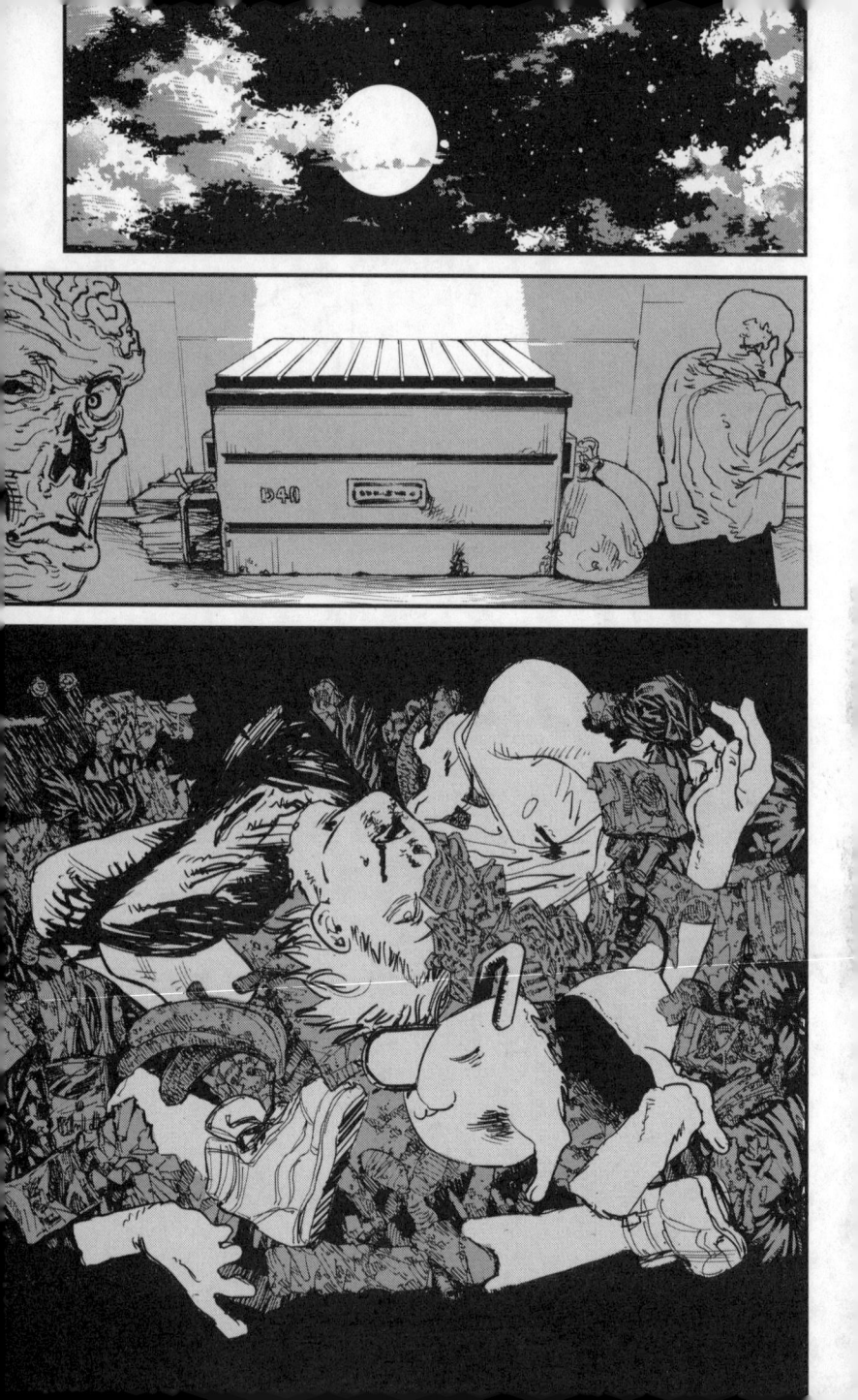
B40

MAKE MY DREAMS COME TRUE FOR ME!

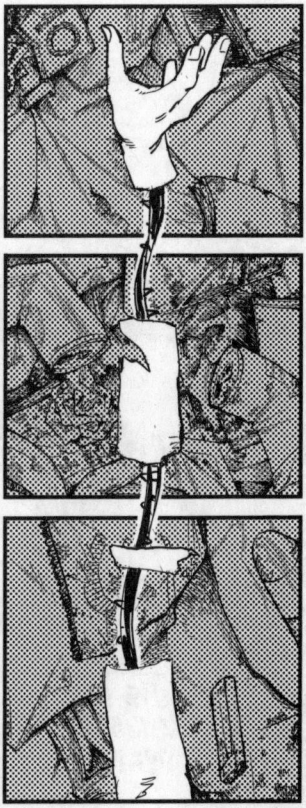

IF YOU'RE ONE OF THEM, THEN...
...I WANNA GIVE MY BODY TO YOU.
YEAH...
AND THEN...
THEN YOU COULD LEAVE THIS TOWN...
IF YOU WAIT TILL AFTER I'M IN THE GROUND, I BET EVEN THE YAKUZA WON'T COME AFTER YOU.
...AND DIE A NORMAL DEATH.
I WANT YOU TO LIVE A NORMAL LIFE...

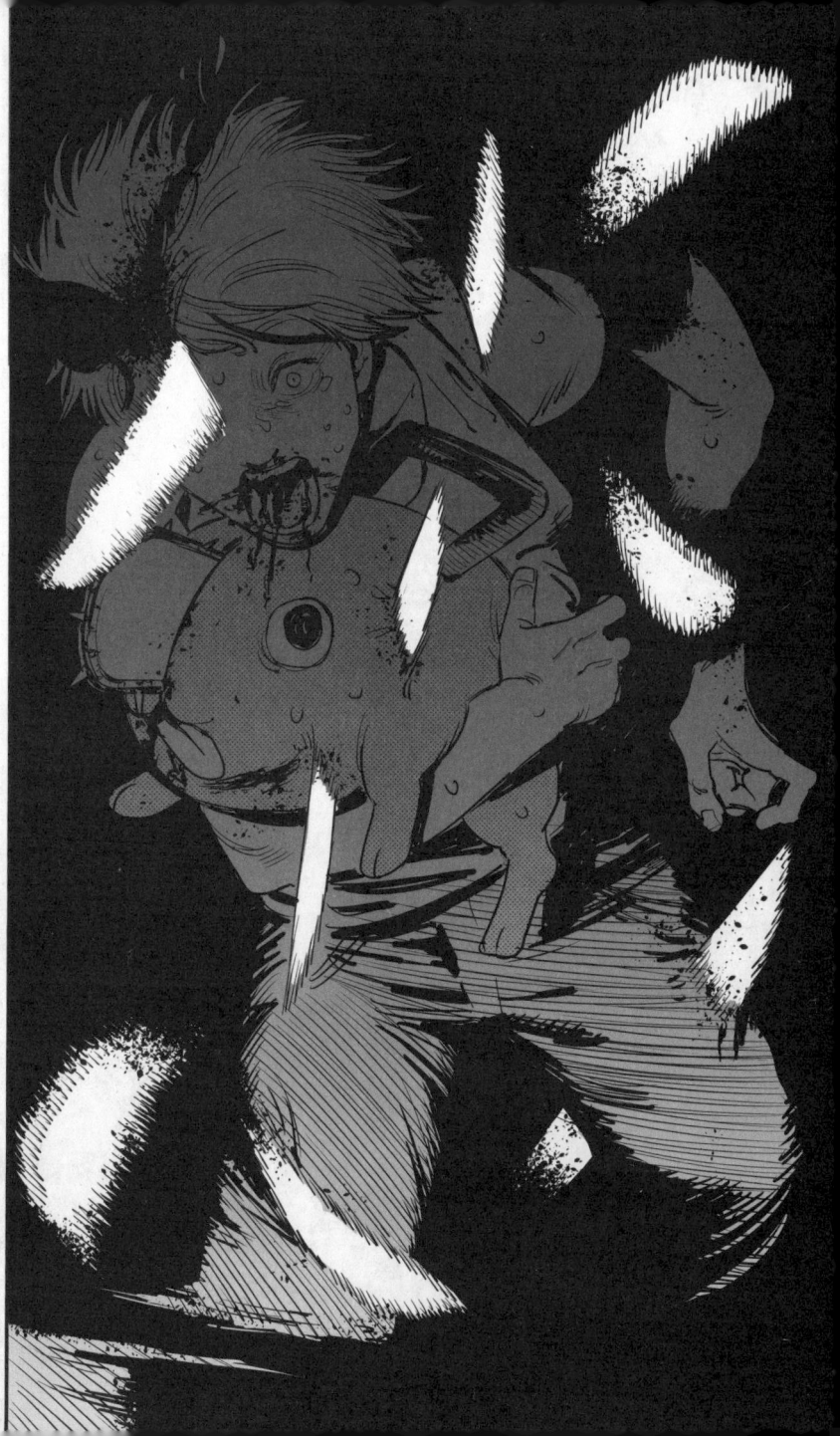

DO I NOT EVEN GET TO HAVE THAT MUCH?
JUST DREAMING OF A NORMAL LIFE WAS ENOUGH FOR ME.

YOU GUYS! CUT HIM INTO PIECES AND DUMP 'IM IN THE GARBAGE!

DEVIL HUNTERS KILL US DEVILS. I HATE THEM!!
SO I KILL THEM!

DAS
H

...THEY BECAME MY SLAVES FREAKIN' WILLINGLY!
WHEN I SAID I'D GIVE THEM MY DEVIL POWER...
HEY, LITTLE DEVIL HUNTERRR!
THESE GUYS! THEY'RE SERIOUSLY STUPID! TOTAL SUCKERS!
CUZ I'M THE ZOMBIE DEVIL!
TOO BAD MY POWER TURNS PEOPLE INTO ZOMBIES!

WHAT WE WANT IS THE DEVILS' POWER...
AND WHAT I WANT IS THE DEATHS...
...OF ALL DEVIL HUNTERS!

SHM
P
SO WE DECIDED TO DO LIKE YOU AND MAKE OUR OWN DEAL WITH A DEVIL.
WE WANTED TO GET STRONGER TOO. TO MAKE MORE MONEY.
WE YAKUZA BOYS...

I DON'T SEE IT...
MAYBE IT HID SOME-WHERE?

A DEVIL SHOWED UP *HERE*, SIR?

OH, UH... YES, SIR...

DENJI, BOY... WE'RE GRATEFUL TO YOU, Y'KNOW.

UH-HUH...

YOU'RE OBE-DIENT LIKE A DOG...
...AND YOU WORK FOR CHEAP TREATS LIKE ONE TOO.

ISH

THING IS... I HATE DOGS. CAN'T STAND THE SMELL.

tak tak
TIME FOR WORK.
DENJI! GOT A DEVIL.
MY MOM... THEY SAID SHE HAD A HEART CONDITION. THAT SHE DIED COUGHING UP BLOOD...
WISH THEY'D AT LEAST LET ME DREAM...

BLEG
Warf ?!
BAM BAM

...AND I'LL FALL ASLEEP IN HER ARMS...
WE'LL PLAY VIDEO GAMES IN OUR ROOM TOGETHER...
I'LL FLIRT AND STUFF WITH A GIRL.
I'LL SPREAD JAM ON SLICED BREAD AND EAT IT WITH YOU.

GOOD DREAM, RIGHT?

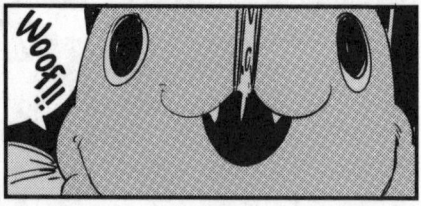
Woof!!!

WHEN I CAN'T SLEEP, I THINK ABOUT MY DEBT, AND THEN IT'S EVEN HARDER TO FALL ASLEEP...

SO HUNGRY I CAN'T SLEEP...

OH, I KNOW...
THIS IS WHAT I'LL DREAM OF WHEN I FALL ASLEEP TONIGHT...

I'LL SAVE YOU... SO YOU SAVE ME.
I DON'T WANNA DIE EITHER...
WILL YOU HIRE ME AS A DEVIL HUNTER, SIR?
SPL
ORCH

BITE ME!
I HEARD THAT IF A DEVIL DRINKS BLOOD, ITS WOUNDS HEAL!
IF YOU DON'T WANNA DIE, THEN BITE ME!
CHO
MP
THIS IS A CONTRACT...
MY BLOOD DOESN'T COME FREE...

YOU'RE HURT...
ARE YOU GONNA DIE TOO...?

A CH-CHAIN-SAW?!
BRM BRM BRM
IT'S A DEVIL!
BRUMM
IF YOU'RE GONNA KILL ME, GET IT OVER WITH!
I'M GONNA DIE ANYWAY!

SSSHHHH
BASTARD HUNG HIMSELF WITHOUT MAKING THIS MONTH'S PAYMENT...
KID... I DON'T CARE IF YOU BEG FOR IT OR WHORE YOURSELF OUT. HAVE 700,000 YEN READY BY TOMORROW.
OR I'LL CUT YOUR CORPSE INTO PIECES AND SELL YOU.

Whiiiiine
AND I'LL PROLLY NEVER GET TO GO OUT WITH A GIRL.
CAN'T ASK A GIRL OVER TO MY RUN-DOWN SHACK, AND I DON'T GOT MONEY FOR A DATE EITHER.
IF DREAMS DO COME TRUE, I WANNA HUG A GIRL BEFORE I DIE...
HHHHSSSN

NOW WE'LL BE ABLE TO EAT FOR THE NEXT THREE DAYS!

ZSSHHHH

WELL, "NORMAL" IS JUST A PIPE DREAM FOR US, ANYWAY.
FEELS LIKE I'LL BE PAYING OFF MY DEBT TILL THE DAY I DIE.

I HEARD SOMETHING RECENTLY...
APPARENTLY, IT'S NORMAL TO EAT YOUR SLICED BREAD WITH JAM ON IT.

HEY, FIDO! I'LL GIVE YOU 100 YEN TO EAT THIS CIG!

AH HA HA HA HA HA!
ぷぷぷ

DOWN THE HATCH!
YOU MEAN IT, SIR?!

bleh

AND REMEMBER, IF YOU RUN AWAY, YOU'LL BE PIG SLOP!
WE'LL CALL YOU AGAIN THE NEXT TIME THERE'S A DEVIL.

WHY ARE WE EMPLOYING SOME KID AS A DEVIL HUNTER?
MORE ACCURATELY, HIS WORTHLESS DEAD DAD'S DEBT.
WE'RE MAKING HIM PAY BACK HIS DEBT TO US.
PLUS, WHAT'S NICE ABOUT DENJI IS HE ALWAYS DOES AS HE'S TOLD.
IS A KID WITH A PET DEVIL REALLY FIT TO BE A DEVIL HUNTER?
NO DEVIL HUNTER WORTH THEIR SALT...
...WOULD DEAL DEAD DEVIL BODIES TO THE YAKUZA, NOW WOULD THEY?

I'M ALREADY DOWN TO 1,800 YEN...
THAT'S FUNNY.

AFTER I USE THIS TO PAY THE WATER BILL...

PLUS THE DEBTS I'VE GOT TO OTHER PEOPLE...

WE HAVE TO LIVE ON THIS FOR THE REST OF THE MONTH...
GOT NOTHING TO EAT AT HOME...

OKAY, POCHITA.
OUR MEAL FOR THE DAY IS A SINGLE SLICE OF BREAD.

IT'LL COME BACK FROM THE SEEDS, SO YOU SHOULD BURN IT.
THIS ONE'S A TOMATO DEVIL, SIR.

YOUR REWARD'S 400,000.
THIS CORPSE'LL FETCH A HEFTY SUM ON THE BLACK MARKET.
GOOD JOB, DENJI.

ONLY 70,000 LEFT FOR ME...

WHICH IS 170,000 AFTER SUB-TRACTING YOUR DEBT AND INTEREST.
WOW, THANKS!

THEN AFTER TAKING OUT THE FINDER'S FEE, ET CETERA...

Chain saw man

Chapter 1: Dog & Chainsaw

KILLING JUST ONE DEVIL...
BROOM
YUP, BEIN' A DEVIL HUNTER IS THE BEST WAY TO MAKE SOME MOOLA.
...NETS ME ABOUT 300,000.

THE KIDNEY I JUST SOLD...
...1,200,000.
TREE-CUTTIN'...
...GETS ME 60,000 YEN A MONTH.
MY RIGHT EYE...
...300,000.
SOLD ONE OF MY NUTS FOR...
HOW MUCH DID IT GO FOR AGAIN?
NOT EVEN 100,000?
THAT BRINGS MY DEBT DOWN TOOOO...
...38,040,000 YEN.
Woof!
OKAY ALREADY, POCHITA. I KNOW!
LET'S GO KILL SOME-THING!

CONTENTS

[1] Dog and Chainsaw 005

[2] The Place Where Pochita Is 061

[3] Arrival in Tokyo 087

[4] Power 111

[5] A Way to Touch Some Boobs 131

[6] Service 151

[7] Meowy's Whereabouts 171

CHAINSAW MAN

1

DOG AND CHAINSAW

Tatsuki Fujimoto